# THE POWER OF THREE

ISBN 978-1-63874-262-3 (paperback)
ISBN 978-1-63874-263-0 (digital)

Christian Faith Publishing, Inc.
832 Park Avenue
Meadville, PA 16335
www.christianfaithpublishing.com

Printed in the United States of America

# THE POWER OF THREE

OMA

Once upon a time, there was a magical garden. It was like any other in the whole world. It was the most beautiful garden you would ever see. It was made magical by all the children in the world. It had trees and bushes and flowers—all kinds of beautiful flowers. In the sky, it had a radiant, shiny rainbow that gave the garden all of its beautiful color. The colors were anything the children could imagine. Inside this garden lived princesses, fairies, and dragons. They all got along very, very well. They loved living there and played with each other all day. Children came and visited every day to play with them.

One day as they were playing, an ogre came along. "Can I play?" he asked.

"Yes," they said.

But he wasn't very nice. He was a mean ogre. He said nasty and hurtful things to the princesses, fairies, and dragons. He would take their things and hit them when they wouldn't do what he wanted. The princesses, fairies, and dragons tried everything they could to be nice, but nothing worked. Pretty soon, they began to become afraid of him because it seemed like he was getting bigger and stronger every day. They decided he had to go, so they banished him from the garden.

Well, this made the ogre very, very mad. So after he left, he decided to put a spell on the garden and the rainbow.

As each day passed, the princesses, fairies, and dragons do notice something. Every day, the rainbow faded a little bit more. The trees, bushes, and flowers began to lose their color. Now they didn't know the ogre put a spell on the garden and the rainbow. So slowly, little by little, the rainbow faded away, and the garden grew dark. This made them very sad. Instead of playing and laughing, they cried. They decided they would search for the rainbow, but when they went to leave, they saw the ogre, he left out an evil laugh, and he said, "You won't let me in, then I won't let you out. I put a spell on the garden and the rainbow, no more color."

This frightened them, and they ran deep into the darkness to the garden. Now it is said that the children all over the world could hear the princesses, fairies, and dragons crying.

They all knew about the magical garden, and their happiness is what kept the rainbow colorful, and everyone knows exactly where it is. To get there, all you had to do was close your eyes, and you will be taken there. But when the crying became so loud in the children's ears, they knew it was their turn to help. So every day, many children went there to try and break the spell. But the ogre that guarded it waited for each child, and he would be so mean that each child went away crying. This made the ogre laugh and grew stronger and bigger each time.

Well, one day, there were three children playing in the backyard. They were cousins, and their names were Emma, Johnny, and Zoey.

There was a picnic going on, so they had come together and were running around, having a good time. Now Emma pretended to be a princess, Johnny wanted to be a dragon and slay the bad guys, and Zoey dreamed of having magical, sparkly wings like a fairy and fly all over the world. But as they played, they could tell something was wrong. Each one of them stopped because they heard something.

"Do you hear that?" said Emma.

"I do," said Johnny.

"They are still crying," said Zoey.

The crying became louder and louder in their ears. This made the three of them sad for the princesses, fairies, and dragons.

"We have to help," said Johnny.

"Yes, it must be our turn to go," said Emma.

"But our moms and dads don't believe us when we tell about the garden," said Zoey.

"Then we won't tell them. We will just go. We have to. They're calling us," said Emma.

"But how can we leave without them seeing?" said Johnny.

"Let's pretend to play hide and seek," said Zoey, "that way they won't look for us."

So the three of them took off and hid. They sat down in the grass and held hands. "Now remember to keep your eyes closed," said Emma. So they kept their hands together and closed their eyes, and off they went to the land where the magical is. They got to the land and had to walk a little way because of the spell the ogre put on it.

When they came close, they could hear the ogre yelling; they stopped because they were afraid.

"Eyes closed, and don't let go of each other's hands," said Zoey.

As they got just about there, they could see the garden. It was very dark, and all the pretty flowers and things were a shade of gray and black. They looked in the sky, but no rainbow. They began to grow sad.

"No, we have to stay happy," said Johnny, so as they sat in the grass, they held each other's hands a little tighter and kept their eyes tightly shut.

Now they were almost there; when the ogre heard them coming, he started yelling, "Who's there?" and stomping his feet to try and scare them away.

17

With determination, they entered the magical zone. "We are sad," Zoey.

The ogre was huge at this point because of all the children he had scared away. He looked down at them and laughed, then said, "Three itty bitty children, you don't stand a chance."

Emma decided to go first, so she stepped forward and confronted the ogre. "Stop being so mean, and break the spell."

"No," said the ogre, and he kicked her.

"Ouch, that wasn't very nice," said Emma.

"I don't want to be nice," said the ogre, and then he pushed her.

This made Johnny mad, and he ran toward the ogre, but the ogre just laughed and knocked him out of the way. Johnny was sure he could win, so he went at him again. This time the ogre shoved him so hard that he fell.

Now it was Zoey's turn; she came forward and yelled very loudly, "LEAVE THEM ALONE!"

The ogre looked down at Zoey and yelled back, "No." Zoey tried again, but the ogre just yelled louder.

"Go away. You can't defeat me. Many have tried, and I have sent them all home," said the ogre.

Now Emma, Johnny, and Zoey were standing together, just staring at the ogre. He just stood there, laughing. They turned around and thought about leaving but heard the crying, then Zoey said, "I have a great idea. We can't win by ourselves, but how about we do it together?"

"Great idea," said Johnny.

"Wonderful," said Emma.

So they held hands as tight as can be and turned back around. They headed straight at the ogre; the ogre saw them and said, "Not you three again. Didn't you have enough the first time?"

They decided no matter he said or did, they would hold hands and say together, "You can't win, we are stronger."

So the ogre tried everything. First, he called them names, but they stayed strong. This surprised the ogre and made him mad. He felt something funny, but was too mad to figure it out, so he tried throwing stones at them, but every one he threw, it missed them. This made him madder than ever. Now Emma, Johnny, and Zoey started to notice he was getting shorter, and there was a small sliver of color in the sky. The ogre did not like that they wouldn't go away, so he kept trying to scare them away, but they just kept together and saying, "We are strong, you can't win."

This went on for some time, but color slowly came back to the rainbow, and the ogre shrank smaller and smaller.

Now the princesses, fairies, and dragons stopped crying, and their color began to return. Now the princesses, fairies, and dragons joined in with telling the ogre, "We are strong, you can't win."

Finally the rainbow was full again, and the beautiful colors returned to the garden. Then the bubble that held everyone inside popped, and the spell was broken. The ogre was sent away and was not allowed back until he changes his ways. The princesses, fairies, and dragons came running out and thanked Emma, Johnny, and Zoey for being strong together and beating the ogre.

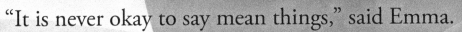

"It is never okay to say mean things," said Emma.

"Or push and shove someone," said Johnny.

"And you should never throw things at someone," said Zoey.

"You are absolutely correct," said everyone in the garden. "But we were afraid," they said. "Many children have tried, and he scared them all, but you three worked together, and he couldn't win. One at a time is hard to win, but the power of three has strength. We will remember this next time, and our garden will never go dark again. We will work together and defeat the bully."

They all played for a little while, and it was time for Emma, Johnny, and Zoey to go back.

"Please come back anytime," said the guardians of the garden.

"Okay," they said. And the garden never went dark again because they learned when confronted with a bully, you have to stay strong, and if you can't do it alone, then get help. And any time a bully or ogre tried again, they stuck together and said, "We are strong, you can't win. We have the power of three."

CPSIA information can be obtained
at www.ICGtesting.com
Printed in the USA
BVHW022303140222
629016BV00001B/7

9 781638 742623